Read All About Sharks

SHARKS OF THE SEAS

Lynn Stone

The Rourke Corporation, Inc.
Vero Beach, Florida 32964

PHOTO CREDITS
©Marty Snyderman: cover, p.4, 6, 9, 12, 15, 19, 20, 22; ©Tom
Campbell: p.7, 13, 18; ©Paul Humann/INNERSPACE VISIONS: p.10; ©
Tsuneo Nakamura/INNERSPACE VISIONS: p.16

Library of Congress Cataloging-in-Publication Data

Stone, Lynn M.
  Sharks of the seas / by Lynn M. Stone
    p. cm. — (Read all about sharks)
  Includes index.
  Summary: Briefly describes some of the more than 350 species of
sharks, including bullhead sharks, mackerel sharks, sawsharks, and
carpet sharks.
  ISBN 0-86593-441-X
  1. Sharks—Juvenile literature. [1. Sharks.]
I. Title II. Series: Stone, Lynn M. Read all about sharks
QL638.9.S849 1996
597'.31—dc20   96–19187
                                       CIP
                                       AC

Printed in the USA

TABLE OF CONTENTS

Sharks of the Seas .5

Sizes and Shapes .6

A Special Kind of Fish 8

Bullhead Sharks 11

Angelsharks .12

Mackerel Sharks 14

Sawsharks 17

Ground Sharks 18

Carpet Sharks 20

Glossary 23

Index 24

SHARKS OF THE SEAS

More than 350 **species** (SPEE sheez), or kinds, of sharks live in the world's oceans. Scientists will probably discover more kinds, too. One of the largest sharks, the megamouth, was not found until 1976.

Scientists divide sharks into eight groups: bullhead sharks, carpet sharks, mackerel sharks, ground sharks, sawsharks, angelsharks, frilled sharks, and dogfish sharks.

Many of these sharks would surprise you by their appearance.

Many sharks don't look the way you expect sharks to look. Sharks come in a great variety of sizes and shapes.

The blue shark, long, slender, and dangerous, is one of the ground sharks.

SIZES AND SHAPES

We expect all sharks to look like great white sharks. Many sharks, though, look almost nothing like their famous great white cousins.

The whale shark, for example, has a wide, blunt mouth instead of a pointed snout. The Pacific angelshark is flattened, like a flounder. Sawsharks have flat, sawlike snouts.

The whale shark's broad, blunt snout moves toward an undersea photographer.

The little horn shark has a spine, or "horn," directly in front of the fin on its back.

The whale shark is the largest of sharks. It can top 40 feet in length. The pygmy shark grows to be less than a foot long!

A SPECIAL KIND OF FISH

Sharks and their relatives, the rays, are different from other fish. Most fish have a skeleton of bone. Sharks and rays have skeletons made mostly of **cartilage** (KART el idj).

Cartilage is softer, lighter, and more flexible than bone. You have cartilage in the frame of your nose.

Sharks don't have a swim **bladder** (BLA der). The bladder, which fills with air like a balloon, helps bony fish stay afloat. Sharks depend upon lightweight oil in their livers for help to stay afloat.

Built differently from bony fish, sharks still swim with ease.

BULLHEAD SHARKS

Bullhead sharks take their name from their broad heads and mouths. They live on reefs and hide in tight spaces between rocks.

The bullhead shark family has eight species. They have been found only in parts of the Pacific and Indian Oceans.

These sharks, unlike some of their larger, fiercer cousins, eat small **prey** (PRAY)—sea urchins and **mollusks** (MAH luhsks).

Bullhead sharks, like freshwater bullhead fish, have spines on the **dorsal** (DOR sul) fins on top of their backs.

The two-foot-long Galapagos bullhead shark has sharp teeth for grasping and flat teeth for crushing.

ANGELSHARKS

The angelshark group has 13 species. These sharks live in waters that range from fairly cold to quite warm. The angelsharks' broad, winglike fins earned them their common name.

Most angelsharks are not large fish. None grows larger than six feet in length. These sharks are so flat-bodied that they can be mistaken for rays.

The flat-bodied angelsharks blend into the sand of ocean bottoms where they ambush prey.

The spotted wobbegong is another bottom-dwelling shark. It belongs to the carpet shark group.

Angelsharks eat small fish and crusty little marine creatures called **crustaceans** (krus TAY shunz).

MACKEREL SHARKS

Mackerel sharks live throughout the oceans. Among the 16 species are several gamefish, including the threshers, great white, and shortfin mako.

By far the largest of the mackerel sharks is the 40-foot-long basking shark. The liver of one basking shark holds over 300 gallons of oil!

Basking sharks eat tiny marine creatures, which they filter through their mouths. Basking sharks often rest at the ocean's surface.

The great white shark is the most famous of sharks and one of the largest mackerel sharks.

SAWSHARKS

Sawsharks are between two-and-a-half feet and four-and-a-half feet long. The five species of sawsharks live on the bottom of warm water.

Sawsharks have toothy, bladelike snouts. They look scary, but they are not considered to be dangerous to people.

Sawsharks probably use their strange snouts like hatchets—to stun or cripple prey.

Like most sharks, sawsharks give birth to live young rather than laying eggs.

Sawsharks make up a small, mild-tempered family of sharks.

GROUND SHARKS

Ground sharks make up the largest family of sharks—197 species. The large, well-known bull, dusky, lemon, and hammerhead sharks belong to this group.

Ground sharks also include the foot-long catsharks and 20-foot tiger sharks. Tiger sharks lose their tiger-stripe markings as they age, but not their tigerlike appetites.

The small, weird-looking swell shark is active at night. It's one of nearly 200 species of ground sharks.

Scalloped hammerhead sharks form huge schools when traveling long distances. Scientists aren't sure why these ground sharks have hammer-shaped heads.

Ground sharks eat bony fish, other sharks, squid, and other marine animals.

Most ground sharks have long, sharp snouts.

CARPET SHARKS

Except for the whale sharks, the 31 species of carpet sharks live mostly near the ocean floor.

Carpet sharks like fairly warm water. Divers often find whale sharks, for example, in the Gulf of Mexico.

The smallest of the carpet sharks is just 12 inches long. The biggest carpet shark—the whale shark—is the world's largest fish.

The nurse shark is a carpet shark, too. Divers commonly see nurse sharks in the Caribbean Sea.

This kind of carpet shark closes its thick eyelids when it's taken out of water. No wonder it's called the blind shark.

GLOSSARY

bladder (BLA der) — a skin sac, or bag, that contains air or liquid in animal bodies

cartilage (KART el idj) — the strong, flexible body tissue that makes up most of a shark's skeleton—and the ridge of a human nose

crustacean (krus TAY shun) — a group of small, shelled (usually) creatures with boneless bodies attached in sections; the lobsters, crabs, shrimp, and their kin

dorsal (DOR sul) — relating to something on or near an animal's back, such as a shark's back fin

mollusks (MAH luhsks) — simple, boneless animals, including many with shells, such as snails, oysters, and clams

prey (PRAY) — an animal that is hunted by other animals for food

species (SPEE sheez) — within a group of closely related animals, one certain kind, such as a *great white* shark.

The sand tiger shark is another kind of carpet shark. It's also called the gray nurse shark.

INDEX

bladder   8

bone   8

cartilage   8

crustaceans   13

divers   20

fins   11

livers   8, 14

prey   11

rays   8

sharks

   angelshark   5, 6, 12

   basking   14

   bullhead   5, 11

carpet   5, 20

dogfish   5

frilled   5

great white   6, 14

ground   5, 18

mackerel   5, 14

megamouth   5

pygmy   7

sawsharks   5, 6, 17

tiger   18

whale   6, 20

species   5